APPLE
RECIPES

"Comfort me with apples"
The Song of Solomon

*with illustrations of
bygone rural scenes
by A. R. Quinton*

SALMON

Index

Cover pictures: *front:* Apple Gathering *by Frederick Morgan*
back: Blossom by the Pond *by Edward W. Waite*
Title page: Blossom at Elmley Castle

Printed and published by Dorrigo, Manchester, England © Copyright

Apple Charlotte

There are many versions of this old recipe, some simple and others very complicated.
This one is easy to prepare and makes a delicious dessert.

1 lb dessert apples, peeled, cored and chopped (weighed after preparation)
1 oz butter   2 oz sugar   2 oz sultanas   Rind of 1 orange
1 egg yolk (if desired)   Slices of stale bread (sliced bread is ideal)
4 oz butter   Caster sugar for sprinkling

Set oven to 375°F or Mark 5. Take an 8 inch pie dish. Melt 1 oz butter in a pan and put in the apples, sugar, sultanas and orange rind. Simmer gently, stirring occasionally until the apples are reduced to pulp. Remove the orange rind and beat to a purée, stirring in the egg yolk, if desired. This will make the purée creamier. Meanwhile melt 4 oz butter in a pan. Remove the crusts from the bread, cut to rectangles, dip one face of each in the melted butter and use to line the base and side of the pie dish, buttered side outwards, overlapping the pieces. When the purée is ready, allow to cool slightly, transfer to the lined dish and smooth out. Cover the purée with bread, buttered side up, overlapping around the edge and brush the joins with melted butter. Put in the oven, cover with a piece of grease-proof paper and bake for 30 minutes. Remove the paper and cook for 10 minutes more to brown the top. Allow to cool slightly, place an oval serving plate over the dish, invert carefully and turn out. Sprinkle with caster sugar and serve warm with cream. Serves 4 to 6.

Blossom time at a Warwickshire Farm

Pork & Apple Pudding

Pork and apples go well together and give this suet pudding a fresh and meaty flavour.

PASTRY
1 lb self raising flour   **A pinch of salt**   **8 oz shredded suet**   **Water to mix**

FILLING
1½ lb raw pork, diced   **1 large cooking apple, peeled, cored and sliced**
Chopped sage to taste   **Salt and pepper**

Butter a 2½ pint pudding basin. Sieve the flour and the salt into a bowl and mix in the suet. Mix to a soft but not sticky dough with just enough cold water. Roll out on a lightly floured surface and use three-quarters of the pastry to line the pudding basin. Put layers of the meat and apple alternately in the lined basin and season well with the sage, salt and pepper. Close the pudding with a lid, using the remaining pastry and wetting the edges. Fold the top of the lining back over the edge of the lid; this will help to seal it. Cover with greaseproof paper and kitchen foil. Steam for 4 hours topping up the water as necessary. Serves 5 to 6.

Apple Slices

This sponge cake recipe is topped with lemon icing and then cut into slices.

1 medium cooking apple, peeled, cored and finely chopped	**Pinch of salt**
	4 oz margarine
Juice of ½ lemon	**4 oz caster sugar**
½ lb self raising flour	**¼ pint milk**
¼ teaspoon baking powder	**1 egg**

ICING

½ lb sifted icing sugar	**3 teaspoons lemon juice**

Set oven to 375°F or Mark 5. Well grease an 11 x 7 inch shallow baking tin. Peel, core and chop the apple finely and mix with the lemon juice. Sift the flour, baking powder and salt into a bowl, rub in the margarine and stir in the sugar. Beat the milk and egg together and stir thoroughly into the mixture together with the chopped apple. Pour the mixture into the tin and spread evenly. Bake for about 30 minutes or until a skewer inserted comes out clean. Make the icing by mixing the icing sugar with the lemon juice and just enough water to make a thick spreading consistency. Pour the icing over the top of the cake whilst still warm and spread evenly. Allow to cool in the tin and when cold cut into 16 slices.

Apple and Potato Cake

This autumn cake would originally have been baked on a griddle but it can equally well be baked in the oven.

1 lb potatoes, weighed after peeling
1 oz softened butter
2 oz flour or 1½ oz flour and
½ oz oatmeal combined
Pinch of salt
2 teaspoons sugar

8 to 10 oz cooking or dessert apples,
peeled, cored and thinly sliced
(weighed after preparation)
A little milk
1 oz butter, cut into flakes
1 oz sugar, white or brown

Pinch of ground ginger or cinnamon

Boil the potatoes in water until tender. Drain *very* well, mash with the butter and allow to cool slightly. Set oven to 400°F or Mark 6. Add the flour, salt and sugar to the mashed potato and knead to form a pliable dough. Divide in half and roll out each half on a lightly floured surface to form two rounds about ½ inch thick. Arrange the apple slices over one round and top with the other, sealing the edges. Place on a greased baking sheet, brush with a little milk and bake for 25 to 30 minutes until golden brown. Remove from the oven and carefully lift off the top. Sprinkle the apple with butter flakes, sugar and spice, replace the top and return to the oven for a further 2 to 3 minutes. Serve at once, cut into slices.

Apple and Bramble Crumble

Apples and blackberries always combine well together.

1 lb cooking apples, peeled, cored and sliced   **8 oz blackberries, washed and drained**

4–6 oz granulated sugar, according to taste

CRUMBLE

4 oz flour   **Pinch of salt**

2 oz porridge oats   **4 oz butter or margarine**

4 oz Demerara sugar

Set oven to 375°F or Mark 5. Mix together the apples and blackberries and put into a pie dish. Add the sugar according to taste and a very little water. For the crumble, put the flour, oats, salt and butter or margarine into a bowl and work together with the hands until the mixture resembles breadcrumbs. Stir in the Demerara sugar and sprinkle the crumble mixture over the fruit. Bake for about 15 minutes and then reduce the temperature to 350°F or Mark 4 and bake for a further 35 to 40 minutes or until the top is lightly browned. Serves 4 to 6.

The Village Cross, Childswickham, Worcestershire

Toffee Apples

Children love this old fashioned treat. Sweet tasting eating apples are the best ones to use.

8 medium size eating apples   **2 oz butter**
8 wooden skewers   **2 teaspoons malt vinegar**
1 lb Demerara sugar   **¼ pint water**
1 tablespoon golden syrup

Wash and dry the apples, remove any stalks and push the skewers into the cores. Prepare the toffee by putting the sugar, butter, vinegar, water and syrup into a large, thick based pan. Heat gently until the sugar dissolves. Bring to the boil and boil rapidly until the temperature reaches the 'soft crack' stage; 280°F/140°C on a sugar thermometer. If a thermometer is not available, test by dropping a little of the toffee into cold water; it has reached the correct stage when it separates into threads which are hard but not brittle. Dip the apples into the toffee, making sure that each one gets a good coating. Stand upright on non-stick baking paper to cool and harden.

Apple Delight

A spicy apple filling covered with a light textured and golden batter topping.

1 lb cooking apples, peeled,
    cored and thinly sliced
2 oz butter
5 oz white wine or cider
4 oz caster sugar
Pinch of freshly grated nutmeg

½ level teaspoon ground cinnamon
2 oz raisins or sultanas
2 oz self raising flour
Pinch of salt
2 medium eggs
2 fl oz double cream

Caster sugar for dusting

Set oven to 350°F or Mark 4. Butter an 8 inch pie dish. Melt the butter gently in a saucepan, add the wine or cider and half the sugar and stir until dissolved. Add the spices, raisins or sultanas and the apple slices. Poach gently until the fruit is almost tender. Put this fruit mixture carefully into the pie dish. Then sieve the flour and salt into a mixing bowl. Add the remaining sugar and the eggs and beat well. Fold in the cream until well blended and pour over the apple mixture. Bake for about 30 minutes until brown and firm. Dust with caster sugar and serve warm with cream. Serves 4.

Cottages at Welford-on-Avon, Warwickshire

Baked Apples with Butterscotch Sauce

Apples, whisky and butterscotch combine to make this a very traditional Scottish recipe.

6 large Bramley apples, cored
4 oz raisins

2 tablespoons whisky
2 tablespoons apple juice

BUTTERSCOTCH SAUCE

4 oz butter
2 tablespoons golden syrup
2 tablespoons black treacle

4 oz soft brown sugar
5 fl oz double cream
3 oz chopped walnuts

Set oven to 350°F or Mark 4. Put the raisins into a bowl with the whisky and leave to soak for 15 minutes. With a sharp knife score around the circumference of each apple to help to prevent it bursting during cooking. Place the apples in an ovenproof dish and stuff with the soaked raisins. Put into the oven and cook for about 35 to 40 minutes. Meanwhile make the sauce. Melt the butter, syrup and treacle in a heavy bottom pan. Add the sugar and stir continuously until it has dissolved and the mixture is bubbling. Remove from the heat and stir in the cream and any leftover whisky from the raisins. Bring back to the boil, remove from the heat and stir in the chopped walnuts. Remove the apples from the oven, pour over the butterscotch sauce and serve immediately. Serves 6.

Apple Dumplings

Marmalade, sultanas and orange rind make the filling; the apples are then individually wrapped in pastry cases.

12 oz shortcrust pastry	**Grated rind of half an orange**
4 teaspoons sugar	**1 dessertspoon marmalade**
4 cooking apples, peeled and cored	**½ oz butter, softened**
2 oz sultanas	**Milk and caster sugar for glazing**

Set oven to 400°F or Mark 6. Roll out the pastry on a lightly floured surface and divide into 4 circles big enough to enclose the apples. Sprinkle each circle with a teaspoon of sugar and set a whole apple in the centre of each. Mix together the sultanas, orange rind, marmalade and butter and divide the mixture between the apples, filling the core holes. Bring the pastry up over the apples, wet the edges and seal firmly. Place the dumplings, upside down, on a greased baking sheet and decorate the tops with any pastry trimmings cut into leaves. Brush the dumplings with milk and sprinkle on a little sugar to glaze. Bake for 10 minutes, then reduce the oven temperature to 350°F or Mark 4 for a further 30 minutes or until the dumplings are golden brown. Serve with a little marmalade warmed to make a sauce, or with custard or cream. Serves 4.

Onion and Apple Pie

*If this savoury pie is to be served cold, 2 to 3 oz of grated or diced Cheddar cheese
can be added at the same time as the onion.*

8 oz shortcrust pastry	Salt and black pepper
2 onions, sliced	½ teaspoon chopped fresh sage
A little oil or butter	2 teaspoons chopped fresh parsley
1 lb cooking apples, peeled,	1 to 2 tablespoons thick double cream
cored and sliced	Beaten egg to glaze

Set oven to 400°F or Mark 6. Butter a 7 inch flan tin. Roll out the pastry on a
lightly floured surface, divide in half and use half to line the tin. Sauté the
onions in the oil or butter until soft, but still transparent, then drain well.
Arrange half the apple slices on the pastry in the tin and top with the onion.
Season well then sprinkle over the herbs. Add the remaining apple slices, then
drizzle over the cream. Top with the remaining pastry, sealing the edges well
and trimming neatly. Make a steam hole in the centre of the pie and decorate
with leaves cut from any pastry trimmings. Brush with beaten egg to glaze and
bake for 30 to 40 minutes until the apples are cooked and the pastry golden
brown. Serves 4 to 6.

Apple and Damson Fool

*Mixing damsons and cinnamon together with apples makes a
delicious autumn pudding.*

½ lb cooking apples, peeled,
    cored and thinly sliced
½ lb damsons
2 oz butter, unsalted
4 oz sugar (or more if preferred)

2 egg yolks
4 tablespoons fresh white
    breadcrumbs
½ pint double cream
1 teaspoon ground cinnamon

Prepare the apples and wash the damsons. Melt the butter in a saucepan, add
the fruit and sugar, just cover with water and simmer until the fruit is soft.
When cooked, cool and purée the fruit, sieve to remove the stones and skins
and add more sugar if preferred. Blend in the egg yolks and the breadcrumbs.
Return to the saucepan and stir the mixture over a low heat until thickened,
then put into a bowl and leave to cool. Meanwhile, whisk the cream lightly
and then fold in to the cooled fruit purée, add the cinnamon and mix well.
When cold, spoon into individual bowls or sundae glasses and serve. Serves 4.

Driving sheep at Cropthorne, Worcestershire

Apple In and Out

Apples mixed in with suet pastry make this a baked pudding with a crunchy top.

8 oz self raising flour	**2 large cooking apples,**
4 oz shredded suet	**peeled, cored and**
2 oz caster sugar	**cut into chunky pieces**
Pinch of salt	**Cold water to mix**

Set oven to 350°F or Mark 4. Butter an 8 inch pie dish. Mix the dry ingredients together in a bowl and stir in the prepared apples. Add just enough cold water to form a soft but not sticky dough. Put into the pie dish, spread out and bake for approximately 45 minutes until golden brown in colour. Serves 4.

Apple Scones

These delicious moist and spicy scones resemble rock cakes when cooked.

8 oz white or wholemeal self raising flour (or mixed)
1 teaspoon ground cinnamon
1 teaspoon baking powder

4 oz butter
2 oz soft brown sugar
2 medium size cooking apples, peeled, cored and finely diced

1 medium egg

Set oven to 375°F or Mark 5. Sift the flour, cinnamon and baking powder together into a mixing bowl. Rub in the butter, stir in the sugar and apple pieces and lastly stir in the egg. Mould into 10 or 12 heaps (as for rock buns) and place on a floured baking sheet. Bake for 20 to 25 minutes. Allow to cool slightly before transferring to a wire rack. Serve sliced in half with butter.

Milking time at Arundel, Sussex

Dessert Apple Cake

A sponge apple pudding from the West Country; delicious served with clotted cream.

6 oz self raising flour	**2 eggs, beaten**
Pinch of salt	**1 cooking apple, peeled, cored**
3 oz butter or margarine	**and sliced**
3 oz sultanas	**½ teaspoon ground cinnamon**
3 oz caster sugar	**1 teaspoon granulated sugar**

Set oven to 400°F or Mark 6. Butter an 8 inch sponge tin. Sieve the flour and salt into a mixing bowl and rub in the butter or margarine. Add the sultanas and the caster sugar. Mix together with the beaten eggs and put into the sponge tin. Peel, core and slice the apple and arrange the slices over the cake mixture. Mix together the ground cinnamon and granulated sugar and sprinkle over the top. Bake for 30 minutes and serve hot or cold with clotted cream. Serves 4.

Swede and Apple Bake

A delicious accompaniment to pork or a supper dish served with crusty bread.

4 oz butter
1 onion, peeled and diced
1 lb swede, peeled and sliced
   into ¼ inch slices

2 medium cooking apples, peeled,
   cored and sliced
Salt and freshly ground black pepper
2 oz fresh breadcrumbs

2 oz grated hard cheese

Set oven to 375°F or Mark 5. Melt 2 oz of the butter in a saucepan and cook the onion gently until soft. Arrange the onion, swede and apple pieces in layers in a greased ovenproof dish, season between each layer and dot with the remaining 2 oz butter. Mix together the breadcrumbs and grated cheese and spread out over the mixture in the dish. Cover with kitchen foil and bake for 1 hour. Remove the cover and continue to cook until the topping is crisp and golden. Serve hot.

Apple Custard Pudding

This is a fruit version of Hasty Pudding, one of the earliest of all old English puddings and so called because it was very quickly made.

1 lb cooking apples, peeled, cored and sliced (weighed after preparation)	1½ oz flour
	1 pint milk, warmed to blood heat
	2 oz caster sugar
3 oz butter	1 teaspoon ground cinnamon

Set oven to 350°F or Mark 4. Butter a 2 to 2½ pint pie dish. First, prepare the apples and put into a saucepan with just a little water. Bring to the boil and simmer until the apples are reduced to a pulp. Melt half the butter in another saucepan, stir in the flour, then gradually add the milk, stirring continually over a low heat until the mixture is thick and smooth. Spoon layers of apple and then of 'custard' into the pie dish, finishing with a layer of 'custard'. Dot with the remaining butter. Mix the sugar and cinnamon together and sprinkle over the pudding. Bake for 20 minutes, then place under a hot grill for 1 to 2 minutes to brown the top. Serves 4 to 6.

Apple Meringue

A very popular family pudding.

1 lb Bramley apples, peeled, cored and cut into pieces

2 eggs, separated

Sugar to taste

Zest of 1 orange

4 oz caster sugar

Set oven to 300°F or Mark 2. Butter an 8 inch pie dish. Separate the egg yolks from the whites. Rinse the apple pieces in cold water, put into a saucepan with sufficient sugar to taste and simmer gently to reduce to a pulp. Allow to cool before mixing in the egg yolks and the zest from the orange. Stir well and put into the pie dish. Make the meringue by whisking the white of eggs stiffly, then add half the caster sugar and whisk again until it holds its peaks; then fold in the remainder of the sugar. Spread over the apple mixture and bake for about 1 hour until the meringue is set. Serve cold with clotted cream. Serves 4.

Cottages at Kersey, Suffolk

Malvern Apple Pudding

A steamed sponge pudding containing finely chopped nutty flavoured Russet apples, currants and brandy; from Worcestershire.

4 oz butter	**4 Russet eating apples, peeled,**
4 oz sugar	**cored and finely chopped**
2 eggs, beaten	**Grated rind of 1 lemon**
4 oz flour	**1 teaspoon lemon juice**
Pinch of salt	**1 oz currants or sultanas**

2–3 tablespoons brandy

Butter a 2½ pint pudding basin. Beat the butter and sugar together in a bowl until light and fluffy, then beat in the eggs. Sift the flour and salt together and fold into the mixture, then add the apples, lemon rind and juice, dried fruit and brandy. Combine well together and turn into the pudding basin. Cover with greaseproof paper and kitchen foil and seal. Place in a saucepan, pour in sufficient boiling water to come half way up the side of the basin, cover and steam for 1½ to 2 hours, topping up the water as necessary. Turn out the pudding on to a warm serving dish and serve with custard, cream or brandy sauce. Serves 4 to 6.

Apple Cheesecakes

Served warm, these little cheesecakes have an apple filling and are topped with a macaroon-like almond mixture.

**8 oz sweet shortcrust pastry
(ideally made with butter)**
4 oz caster sugar
3 oz ground almonds
The *unbeaten* white of 1 large egg
½ oz ground rice

A few drops of vanilla essence
**4 oz apple pulp, sieved and weighed
after preparation**
1 teaspoon melted butter
2½ oz Madeira or sponge cake crumbs
Sifted icing sugar for dusting

Set oven to 350°F or Mark 4. Grease and flour 10 to 12 tartlet tins. First make the apple pulp by boiling about one large cooking apple, peeled, cored and chopped, in just a very little water until soft. Roll out the pastry on a lightly floured surface and use to cut out and line the tins. Mix the sugar, ground almonds and ground rice together in a bowl with the unbeaten egg white and vanilla essence, then set aside. Mix the apple pulp with the melted butter and the cake crumbs, divide between the tartlet tins and top each one with the almond mixture. Bake for about 25 minutes until golden. Remove from the tartlet tins and serve warm, dusted thickly with sifted icing sugar.

Blossom time at Norton, Worcestershire

Spicy Apple Sauce Cake

A spicy cake which contains sultanas and glacé cherries, the apple first being cooked to a pulp. This makes a moist cake and hence a good 'keeper'.

2 or 3 cooking apples, peeled, cored and sliced
5 oz butter, softened   5 oz soft brown sugar   2 eggs, beaten   8 oz self-raising flour
1 teaspoon ground mixed spice   ½ teaspoon ground cinnamon   Pinch of salt
2 oz sultanas   2 oz glacé cherries, halved   Grated rind of half a lemon
1 dessertspoon Demerara sugar for sprinkling

Cook the apples with a very little water until soft, then sieve to produce a smooth purée; there should be 4 to 5 oz. Allow to cool. Set oven to 350°F or Mark 4. Grease and line a 7 inch round cake tin. Cream together the butter and sugar in a bowl until light and fluffy, then beat in the eggs, a little at a time. Sift together the flour, spices and salt and stir into the mixture. Add the dried fruit. Mix the lemon rind with the apple purée and fold into the mixture. Put into the tin and smooth the top. Sprinkle a dessertspoon of Demerara sugar over the cake to give a crunchy topping. Bake for about 1¼ to 1½ hours or until golden brown and springy to the touch and a skewer inserted comes out clean. Cool in the tin for 15 minutes, then turn out on to a wire rack.

Apple Pasties

These individual puff pastry apple turnovers are useful as a cold snack.

**2 large cooking apples, peeled,
  cored and chopped**
6 oz sugar
3 cloves

A walnut of butter
8 oz puff pastry
White of egg for glazing
Caster sugar for sprinkling

Set oven to 400°F or Mark 6. Put the apple pieces into a saucepan with the sugar, cloves and butter. Cook very slowly, with the lid on, so that the apple only cooks and does not brown or burn. Then leave to get quite cold. Take out the cloves. Roll out the pastry ⅛ to ¼ inch thick on a lightly floured surface and cut out rounds the size of a saucer. Put a tablespoon of the cooked apples on each round of pastry, dampen the edges and fold over in the form of a Cornish pasty. Crimp the edges with the finger and thumb. Brush over with white of egg and sprinkle with sugar. Place on a greased baking sheet and bake until golden brown. Transfer from the baking sheet to a wire rack to cool.

Apple, Raisin and Cider Teabread

A good, fruity, apple flavoured teatime treat.

8 oz self raising flour	**1 medium cooking apple, peeled,**
¼ teaspoon salt	**cored and finely chopped**
1 level teaspoon mixed spice	**3 oz raisins soaked in**
4 oz butter	**2 tablespoons cider**
3 oz soft brown sugar	**2 medium eggs**

GLAZE

2 oz soft brown sugar	**2 tablespoons cider**

Set oven to 350°F or Mark 4. Butter a 2 lb loaf tin. Sieve the flour, salt and spice into a bowl and rub in the butter until the mixture resembles fine breadcrumbs. Stir in the sugar, chopped apple and raisin/cider mixture. Add the eggs and mix well. Put the mixture into the loaf tin and bake for approximately one hour until golden and firm and when a skewer inserted comes out clean. Turn out to cool on a wire rack. Boil the glaze ingredients together in a pan for 3 or 4 minutes and brush over the warm loaf. Serve sliced, plain or buttered.

Apple Pudding

This warming winter recipe dates from the 19th century.

4 cooking apples, peeled, cored and sliced	**4 oz shredded suet**
½ lb flour	**Grated rind and juice of 1 small lemon**
¼ teaspoon baking powder	**2 oz butter**
Pinch of salt	**4 oz sugar**
	2 heaped tablespoons apricot jam

Butter a 2 pint pudding basin. Sift the flour, baking powder and salt together into a bowl, then rub in the suet and just sufficient cold water to make a firm dough. Roll out on a lightly floured surface and use two-thirds to line the pudding basin, reserving the remaining pastry for the lid. Cook the apples together with the lemon rind and juice, butter, sugar and jam until soft, but still holding their shape. Allow to cool a little then spoon into the basin. Cover with the remaining suet pastry, wetting and sealing the edges well. Cover with buttered greaseproof paper and seal with kitchen foil. Place in a steamer and steam over a saucepan of boiling water for 1½ to 2 hours, topping up the water as necessary. Before serving, wrap a white table napkin around the basin and serve the pudding straight from this, accompanied by cream or custard. Serves 4 to 6.

Orchard beside the River Gipping, Suffolk

Apple and Parsnips

In this recipe apples are combined with parsnips to make an appetising accompaniment to roast pork.

**1 lb apples (cooking or dessert),
    peeled, cored and sliced**
1 lb parsnips, peeled and chopped

A good size walnut of butter
**Pinch each of ground cinnamon,
    cloves and nutmeg**

Pepper

Rinse the apples in cold water, put into a saucepan and cook slowly under they are soft. Boil the parsnips in another saucepan until they also are quite soft. Drain the parsnips well and combine with the apples, mashing them together until smooth. Stir in the butter, pepper and spices and re-heat through, if necessary, before serving with roast pork. Apples and Parsnips is a sauce which also goes well with roast duck.

Nut and Apple Cake

This coffee and nut sponge cake has an apple and apricot jam filling.

4 oz butter	4 oz self raising flour
4 oz caster sugar	Pinch of salt
2 eggs, separated	1 teaspoon instant coffee
1½ oz roasted ground hazelnuts	1 tablespoon warm milk

FILLING

1 lb Cox's Orange Pippin apples, peeled, cored and sliced

2 tablespoons apricot jam **Grated rind and juice of ½ lemon**

2 oz melted plain chocolate or sifted icing sugar for topping

Set oven to 375°F or Mark 5. Grease and line a 8 inch round cake tin. Soften the butter in a bowl, add the sugar and beat until fluffy. Add the egg yolks, nuts, sifted flour and salt. Dissolve the coffee in the milk and add to the mixture; then fold in the stiffly beaten egg whites. Turn into the tin and bake for about 25 minutes until firm and a skewer inserted comes out clean. Turn out on to a wire rack and leave to cool. Meanwhile peel, core and slice the apples and place in a pan with the jam and the rind and juice of ½ lemon. Cover and cook gently until soft, then allow to cool. Split the cake in half and fill with the apple mixture. For the top of the cake, either spread with 2 oz of melted plain chocolate or sprinkle with sifted icing sugar.

Feeding chickens at Harvington, Worcestershire

Chicken and Apple Cheesebake

An unusual supper dish with a crispy topping finished with buttered apple slices.

12 oz cooked chicken, diced
5 Cox's Orange Pippins
4 oz butter
½ pint white sauce

4 oz grated Cheddar cheese
4 tablespoons toasted white
 breadcrumbs
Salt and black pepper

Set oven to 400°F or Mark 6. Butter a shallow ovenproof dish. Peel, core and slice 4 of the apples and fry them gently in the butter. Arrange the chicken pieces in the bottom of the dish and put the apple slices on top. Make ½ pint of white sauce. Mix 3 oz of the cheese into the white sauce and pour over the apples. Season. Mix the breadcrumbs with the remaining 1 oz of cheese and sprinkle over the sauce. Cut the remaining apple into rings (cored but unpeeled), toss in the leftover apple butter and arrange neatly on top of the dish. Bake for 20 to 30 minutes until crisp and golden. Serves 4.

Blackberry and Apple Pudding

The fruits of hedgerow and orchard are combined into this variation of Summer Pudding; a lovely dessert to serve on a brilliant autumn day.

1 lb cooking apples, peeled, cored and thinly sliced
1 lb blackberries, washed and drained

1 pint water
6 oz sugar
8–12 slices white bread, crusts removed

Simmer the fruit in the water until just tender. Stir in the sugar until dissolved. Set aside to cool. Cut a circle of bread to fit the base of a 2 lb pudding basin, then cut wedge shaped slices of bread and line the sides of the basin. Fill one third of the basin with the fruit mixture, cover with another circle of bread then add more fruit and a further circle of bread. Add more fruit until the basin is almost full then add a final circle of bread. Cover with a saucer which fits the top of the basin and place a weight on top. Leave in the refrigerator for 24 to 48 hours. Turn out carefully on to a serving dish. Serve with whipped cream. Any left-over fruit mixture can be strained and the juice poured over the pudding when ready to be served. Serves 6 to 8.

Apple and Cheese Pie

Layers of apple and cheese make this pie an ideal supper dish.

1½ lbs cooking apples, peeled, cored and thickly sliced	Small pinch of grated nutmeg
3–4 oz granulated sugar	½ cup of water
3–4 cloves	4 oz hard cheese, sliced
	6 oz puff or shortcrust pastry

Set oven to 425°F or Mark 7. Butter an 8 inch pie dish. Using half the apples, put a layer into the dish. Sprinkle half the sugar over the apples. Lay the remaining apples on top and push the cloves into some of the apple slices. Add all the remaining sugar, the grated nutmeg and the water and make a final layer with the cheese slices. Roll out the pastry on a lightly floured surface and use to cover the dish. Trim, brush with a little milk and bake for approximately 40 to 45 minutes until golden brown. Serves 4 to 6.

Pippin Pie

This pie is unusual in that the apples are put whole into the pie dish. Cox's Orange is the best known pippin apple.

6 eating apples (preferably pippins) peeled and cored
Almonds
Sultanas

1 piece of cinnamon stick per apple
1 or 2 cloves per apple
Grated rind and juice of 1 large orange
8 oz shortcrust pastry

Set oven to 375°F or Mark 5. Butter a large pie dish. Peel and core the apples, leave whole and arrange in the pie dish. Fill each apple centre with a few almonds, sultanas and a piece of cinnamon stick. Push cloves into each apple and sprinkle with the grated rind from the orange. Squeeze the orange and pour the juice over the apples. Roll out the pastry on a lightly floured surface, cover the dish, trim the edge and bake for approximately 35 to 40 minutes until the apples are cooked and the pastry is brown. Serves 6

Cottage garden at Groombridge, Kent

Apple Tart

Dessert apples are used in this caramelised upside down version of an apple pie.

1 lb dessert apples (preferably Cox's) peeled, quartered, cored and sliced thinly
3 oz soft brown sugar

1 teaspoon ground cinnamon or ¼ teaspoon ground cloves
8 oz sweet shortcrust pastry
1 oz melted butter, for brushing

Set oven to 350°F or Mark 4. Brush an 8 inch flan tin (preferably without a flange) with melted butter. Line the base with greaseproof paper and brush again with butter. Cover the base with the sugar, spread out evenly and sprinkle over the cinnamon or cloves. Arrange the apple slices, overlapping neatly in circles to cover the base of the tin completely. Roll out the pastry on a lightly floured surface to about an 8 inch circle, cover the apples, press down gently and trim. Cook in the oven for about 30 to 40 minutes until the pastry is golden brown. Set aside to cool. When cold, loosen the edge with a knife, cover with a serving plate and invert carefully to turn out, leaving the pastry base underneath. Remove the tin and paper and serve cold with double cream or custard. Serves 4 to 6.

Buttered Apples

This quickly made farmhouse pudding from Herefordshire would usually be served with Cider Sauce.

1 lb cooking apples, weighed after peeling and coring
6 oz sugar

6 oz butter
3 thick slices stale bread, crusts removed and cut into cubes

A little extra sugar (optional)

CIDER SAUCE
1 pint cider   ¼ lb sugar   2 to 3 oz butter

Cut the apples into slices and roll in the sugar until completely coated. Melt half the butter in a frying pan and fry the apples until golden brown and soft. Keep warm on a serving dish. Melt the remaining butter in the pan and fry the bread cubes until golden brown and crisp. Lightly combine with the apples, sprinkle over a little extra sugar, if desired and serve at once, accompanied by hot Cider Sauce or whipped cream. Serves 4 to 6.

CIDER SAUCE: Simmer the cider and sugar together in a pan, to form a light syrup, stirring from time to time. Cut the butter into small pieces and whisk into the mixture. Pour into a sauce boat and serve at once.

Blossom time at Dorsington, Worcestershire

Caramelised Apple Cream

A variation of a classic dessert; apple purée with sultanas covered with a rich cream mix and topped with caramelised sugar.

1 lb dessert apples, peeled, cored and chopped
2 tablespoons lemon juice   1 oz sultanas   1 pint double cream
1 cinnamon stick   3 egg yolks   2 oz caster sugar
6 dessertspoons Demerara sugar

Prepare 6 large ramekin dishes. Put the chopped apple and the lemon juice into a pan with just a very little water and heat gently, stirring, until reduced to a pulp. Stir in the sultanas and set aside to cool. Put ¾ pint of the cream into another pan with the cinnamon stick and bring to the boil. Take off the heat and set aside to infuse for about 10 minutes then remove the cinnamon stick. In a bowl, whisk the egg yolks with the caster sugar until it becomes pale then whisk in the remaining cream. Stir this into the warm cream in the pan and cook over a moderate heat, stirring, until thickened. Divide the apple/sultana mixture equally between the 6 ramekin dishes and cover with the cream mixture. Leave to cool, then chill in the refrigerator. Meanwhile, turn on the grill to its highest setting to get really hot; a fierce grill heat is needed. Cover the top of each ramekin with a spoonful of Demerara sugar and put under the grill for 2 to 3 minutes until the sugar melts and bubbles. Set aside to cool, then chill for an hour or so until required. Serves 6.

Apple Pancakes

This supper dish needs well-flavoured dessert apples for the best result; Cox's are ideal. Cooking apples will require extra sugar.

4 apples, peeled, cored and sliced into thin rings	**4 egg yolks**
4½ oz flour	**½ pint milk**
1 teaspoon baking powder	**¼ pint double cream**
1 tablespoon icing sugar	**1 teaspoon vanilla essence**
Salt to taste	**Butter for frying**
	Icing sugar for dusting

Sift the flour, baking powder, icing sugar and salt into a bowl, make a well in the centre and mix in the egg yolks. Then mix in the milk, cream and vanilla essence and beat vigorously to make a smooth batter. Melt a little butter in an omelette pan, swirl to cover completely and pour in sufficient batter to coat the entire surface. As the underside starts to set, press a few slices of apple into the surface. Allow the pancake to brown underneath and firm up on top then place a buttered plate over the pan, invert carefully and slide the pancake back into the pan to finish browning. Serve immediately, apple side up and dusted with icing sugar. Repeat to use up the batter and apples. Serves 4.

Apple Gingerbread

An unusual variation of a traditional gingerbread.

½ lb cooking apples, peeled, cored and sliced
Sugar to taste
¼ lb golden syrup
3 oz butter

3 oz Demerara sugar
6 oz self raising flour
1 teaspoon ground ginger
¼ teaspoon ground cloves
1 egg

Set oven to 350°F or Mark 4. Butter an 8 inch x 6 inch baking tin. Rinse the apple pieces and put into a pan with sufficient sugar to taste. Stew gently until tender, then mash and cool. In a separate pan melt the syrup and butter and Demerara sugar together gently until dissolved. Leave to cool. Sift the flour, ginger and cloves into a bowl and make a well in the centre. Stir the egg into the syrup mixture, pour into the flour and beat well. Stir in the mashed apples and continue to beat all well together. Turn into the tin and cook for 30 minutes until firm and a skewer inserted comes out clean. Leave to stand for a few minutes in the tin before turning out to cool on a wire rack; cut into slices.

METRIC CONVERSIONS

The weights, measures and oven temperatures used in the preceding recipes can be easily converted to their metric equivalents. The conversions listed below are only approximate, having been rounded up or down as may be appropriate.

Weights

Avoirdupois	Metric
1 oz.	just under 30 grams
4 oz. (¼ lb.)	app. 115 grams
8 oz. (½ lb.)	app. 230 grams
1 lb.	454 grams

Liquid Measures

Imperial	Metric
1 tablespoon (liquid only)	20 millilitres
1 fl. oz.	app. 30 millilitres
1 gill (¼ pt.)	app. 145 millilitres
½ pt.	app. 285 millilitres
1 pt.	app. 570 millilitres
1 qt.	app. 1.140 litres

Oven Temperatures

	°Fahrenheit	Gas Mark	°Celsius
Slow	300	2	150
	325	3	170
Moderate	350	4	180
	375	5	190
	400	6	200
Hot	425	7	220
	450	8	230
	475	9	240

Flour as specified in these recipes refers to Plain flour unless otherwise described.